I'm glad I wrote it down

Chris Rogers

Presentation by *BookLeaf Publishing*

Web: www.bookleafpub.com

E-mail: info@bookleafpub.com

ISBN: 9789357214575

First edition 2022

*To Ellie, for telling me this existed and
making me write it down.*

A book of Poems

This book is full of poems
Some are short, some are long
Some are more like stories
And some are more like songs

Each of them has meaning
Whatever 'meaning' really means
Be they serious or silly
Built from reality, or dreams

Sometimes they follow patterns
Sometimes they sort of don't
Most of the time they rhyme but not always

Every one represents a moment
Of thought, or soul, or time
Where something stirred within me
Which I had to release in rhyme

They're not always soft and pretty
Not all a tour de force
But did I need to write them
The answer, of course; of course.

Love

Love is a story not for me to read
Hope is a glory from a planted seed
Tell me desires that you hold to tight
Give me the moments that you save for night

I ain't nothing but a simple man
Doing my best with gods given plan
Weary to walk but here it is I stand
Save me from all the things I don't understand

I ain't got no problems but I'm worried just the
same
Too many thoughts clogging my up my brain
Soothe all my anger with the faintest smile
Take both my hands and just stay a while

Love is the paper on which we bleed
Signed on the line with want and need
Dark are the hours that you call you own
Hard is the path where we're tossed and blown

I'm nothing more than a simple man
Trying my best but it's out of hand
Too weary to walk, or to give a damn
Trying my best to better understand

Love is a story that's mine to tell
You know your parts, as it's yours as well
Deep in your heart where you hide your pain
I'll rest with you baby, till we begin again

Home

Home is a person, not a place
The well worn memory of a face

Not your favourite chair
Or warming hearth

But the bright eyes of a smile
And the echo of a laugh

Home is a person, not walls and things
Not pictures or postcards or shiny gold rings

It's the hands to hold
And the arms to embrace

The lips to caress
And the hearts to make race

Home is a person, not a writ or a deed
Not just wanting, but longing, an enduring need

The unashamed tears
The safety from harm

The gentle content
And resonant calm

Home is a person, not a city or town
Not locked in place or forever tied down

There is no set contract
That's written in stone

Wherever you're loved
Thats where you are home

You

Your eyes are not just brown
But are marked with red and gold
They're like autumn leaves that fall
And fires embers in the cold

Your hair is soft and silken falls like honey cross
your breast
Wherein my heart and my affection
Are kept safe within their nest

You walk as if we're weightless
Born to float along the air
Free from heavy thought or sadness
Ne'er a slave to anger or despair

Your touch is cool as water
Soothes all doubt and eases pain
It cures the wounds of everyday
And clears the skies of clouds and rain

Your embrace is fire and lightning
A storm that rocks me to my soul
It is safety and contented
And the only time I'm whole

You are flawed and you are stubborn
You are graceful and sublime
You've been hurt and you've been broken
And you're perfect and you're mine

Love and Thunder

The sordid seance sits secluded
Screaming of what's and when's
As frightful friends forage for fruitless
Means unto their ends

The old guard sits unmoving
Yet unwavering and unafraid
Staring out across the wild
Scorched remains of what they've made

I stand and stare into what's there
And see what's not to be seen
The missing space and emptiness
That keeps the land serene

The scarred and battered general stands
On lands he bled to keep
He keeps his watch and wonders why
Nought eludes him save for sleep

Tears of blood like raindrops fall
From the martyrs shaking mind
Burnt by broken promises
Of the unjust and unkind

The blonde haired Jesus drunken fool
Stumbles through truths and lies
With each new phrase he begs and prays
For an escape from the noose he ties

Whilst one hand shakes the other breaks
Into a fist with which only to blow
At the smiling face with no remorse
Of the lives and the sins it has sown

And I will not go
So willingly
Into the darkness and the black
Not whilst life still fills me with love and
thunder

Aggressive politicians scream and cower
From the crowds
When contradicting pledges of allegiance
Aren't allowed

They're scared to face the people whom
They preach to represent
For they taste the tar and sawdust
The exude when they repent

I strain to hear the promises
The confusion and the gall
Of each molesting invasive thought

They thought they should share with all

Is time to spare the time to keep
Or to weep of the moments lost
When freedom comes with bloated men
Is it even worth the cost

I'd rather see no other than me
Stand alone upon the prow
Than follow with blind exuberance
The men of here and now

The reckless rally to the deaf
And they lead the blind to war
And sit in comfort of their homes
To complain of what they saw

But I will not
So willingly go
Into the darkness or the black
Not whilst life still fills my heart with wonder

The bent down servant now
Is breaking her back to spy
Upon the golden lavish life
The diamonds, and the sky

The next law passed is questioned more
Than was ever dared to dream

And fists are raised higher than
They may even yet still seem

And all in all it's worth the call
To arms and to the end
It's means unto a change and change
Is the only way we mend

I'll stand and I'll be counted
Against the darkness and the black
Whilst life still pumps through my heart
There'll be no turning back.

Temple Meads Station

At Temple Meads station I sat down and wept
Heavy sat the cloud of the secrets I'd kept
Blasphemous beliefs of an endangered soul
Unbridled and ravenous and out of control

Without a within and coming unstuck
Untidy in life, love, and giving a fuck
Eyes leaden and leaving no question unspoke
Upon lies upon tears upon nothingness choked

The shadows pass by and pass over a grave
Sat within it I ponder the mistakes freely made
Had I the thought or presence of mind at the
time
Would I undo mistakes of a life unrefined

I held you. I hold you. Forever still now
Could I ever let go could I ever know how
You're the error of judgement that judges all sin
From the start to the finish. Where I end and
begin.

Rain falls around me beneath the blue skies
Through the stories I tell and the beautiful lies
Why let any truth spoil such good a tale

The grasp on reality becoming so frail

Drinking and drunk and decrepit near death
Berated and broken and bent out of breath
Bones cold. Heart broken. Eyes lifeless and
hollow
Self righteous, self loathing. Sun kissed by
sorrow

Laughing and loving and living to full
Unable to escape the nights lonely pull
A smile lasts only as long as it's seen
Like the fading memory of a half woken dream

The life and the lovers and the limitless lie
Burning through years and tears that you'd cry
Pretending you're fine and knowing you're not
Showing only your beauty and never your rot

Sickly and starving and desperate and sad
Life won't treat you poorly it'll just treat you
bad
Broken by silence and the few hours slept
By Temple Meads station, I fell down and wept

On the shelf

A row of books
All worn and warped,
their spines bent backwards
by eager hands

Their pages turned
And turned again
By a mind that yearns
to understand

Through other worlds
and countless lives
The thirst for more
The only demand

Pages creased
A corner bent
A certain passage
Strikes a chord

Margins defaced
By freeing thought
A tattooed page
Is never flawed

So much choice
So much to read
Always searching
Never bored

There's a little space
There at the end
For more
I shouldn't buy

Too many still
Lay un begun
Though I'll get to them
If I try

Until then what
Could be the harm
Of more books
On the shelf to lie

Just too much to read
Too little time

Slippers

Grey tartan slippers
Worn and old
Keep my toes safe
From the cold

Old at heart
But free to roam
Warm and comfy
Round my home

I'd happily end up one day
Like my slippers, old and grey

Clouds

I'm sat here wasting my time
Painting faces with the clouds
Minding nobody's business but mine
I'm sure that's allowed

Won't you come and sit with me
Watch the day drift by
Smile and wave to the sun and the sea
We've no cause to cry

Leaves are green and the sky is blue
Grass is soft to the touch
I want to spend this time with you
Because you mean so much

I see my reflection in your eyes
And it makes me smile
We watch the flowers and the butterflies
As they play chase for a while

Missing You

I miss the way your hands held mine
And every time you'd stroke my cheek
at night
I miss you arms around me
And surrounding me with love until
the light

I miss the beating of your heart
And work of art that is the smile
on your face
I miss the softness of your skin
And there's nothing of you that I
can replace

I miss the hours in the morning sun
When day has just begun lying and watching
as you sleep
I miss your gentle breathing
And believing that my life was
complete

I miss your ups and all your downs
And being around to pick you up off
the floor
I miss your laugh and your sigh

And I don't know why that I'm not enough
anymore

Missing all of you hurts me so much
But of one thing I am sure
Nothing hurts as much as knowing
You don't miss me
anymore

House of Mirrors

Prime minister is riding
In a car with no brakes
The guy driving it is the president
Of the United States
They're both screaming out the window
That it's for all our sakes
And it can't end now that they have begun it

I try to do good but
I do well at best
I'm no saint, I'm a man,
I'm just like all the rest
I must admit, I feel relieved
To get that off my chest
Now here's the stone with my name carved upon
it

You stand tall, but you're small
You're exactly like me
You'll be brushed aside, like dust
Into history
For they held you and they forced you
To see reality
And the weight of it all fell down on you

I've been kicked about
And bastardised
Had my heart ripped out
and not cauterised
I've known pain and I've had love
But not realised
But where im flesh and bone you're see through

Some men speak behind my back
And others to my face
Some men spit in my direction
And they call me a disgrace
But all these men are welcome
For they all have their place
And I'll not change, and still voice, my opinion

Your skin shimmers like silver
Your hair is golden thread
Your voice rolls and flows like water
As it calls me to your bed
But your eyes are red like fire
And your heart is made of lead
And I'm a slave under your dominion

Ask that man 20 questions
And disregard all his replies
He's so eloquent and polite
In the way in which he lies
That you think you understand

What it is that he implies
But he's like the wind when you press him for an
answer

A man in a suit
Suggests things suitable to think
And another warns me of the things
I should not eat or drink
Then next week tells me different
Just to push me to the brink
Well is there anything left that won't give me
cancer?

Now I don't know whether
To weather the storm
Or whether or not it's better forgot
That we're all feeling so torn
Between searching, or accepting
That it's all forlorn
But im desperate for some kind of reason

So you leave me here
To fend for myself
With these medicines and potions
Which are 'good for my health'
And these maniacs and scholars
With their trophies on the shelf
And all dressed in the clothes of next season

The politicians and prostitues
Are playing the same game
The devil holds the dice
And he knows them all by name
They're all sat around the table
Deciding on who to blame
And the finger points to all, and yet to no one

So leave me here
Lost inside my head
Searching out the answers
Now that I've been left for dead
With the power mad junkies,
and the life long sinners
With God, faith, and science, in a house of
mirrors

Without

Without, without, without
A hope, a cause, a purpose
Weighed down by memories of dreams that feed
us just to hurt us.

I feel I'm losing track of time
Distracted by thoughts which I worry aren't
mine
Forcing through feelings just to show them I'm
fine

I fear I'm losing my sense of what's real
The vodka bottle grows in its appeal
The disillusion harder now, to conceal

But don't hold on to something too hot to touch
The ice in the glass will only help you so much
Burn out and explode? Seems the ultimate rush

The anger will always subside
Pain passes after a while
But the pictures which always make me cry are
the ones that made me smile

Sleep

8 hours sleep is more than enough
A third of your day?! Asleep?
A third asleep
A third at work
A third actually living

Am I supposed to quietly surrender
All of my daylight? For you?
Trapped in the chair
Stealing away moments
When the years grow less forgiving

I wish I'd tried harder at school
Or at least, just tried harder. Somewhere
Escapes don't escape
They just pull at the chain
And the chain has never been giving

That silence is all I can hear
At the end of the question. Still shifting.
No answer to come
And there's no answer that fits
As no answer could ever be fitting

Wanting

Encumbered often with fleeting thought
Of dreams and plans all come to nought
And sweet innocence, who's stay, too short
Weighs heavy on the conscience

The truths of broken lier's warns
That heaviness of falsehood swarms
When the evidence of mistrust dawns
Brought high before the conference

Three words spoken much, but rarely meant
Around our lives entwined and bent
In past tense, burns what was freely lent
And leaves but numb indifference

What a way to be left wanting

A child's laughter brings forth a smile
That lingers longer than a while
In memory, where only age defiles
The crispness of a moment

Eyes that sparkle, or shine bright
Into depths which have ne'er seen light
Awaken dreams best kept at night

And burst with life too potent

A brief cascade of far too much
Assaults the sight and taste and touch
Descending notes of fear are such
Needlessly urgent

What a way to be found wanting

Today

I think I love you
But I fear I've forgotten how
Maybe I don't remember what it's supposed to
be
Maybe I can only remember what it was before

I think I'm stuck
Comparing everything now to then
What is missing that I'm expecting to appear
As there's a gap in all of this I can't ignore

I think I'm afraid
Have I felt it all before
Have I used up all the feelings there are
Something isn't right and I wish I wanted more

I think I'm just wrong
Stuck sort of stranded and scared
Always feeling just that little out of place
Always telling myself I'm fine but never
sounding sure

If we're all just lost and flailing
With no idea of where we're going
Always afraid of others thoughts

Of what to the world it is we're showing

Can we not just drop the mask
Release that internal bugging
If I have to be the first to say
World. Today I'm struggling

Night

Silence rolls around the room
Encompasses the cold hard tomb
Of joys spent wastefully, and still
The empty space, the silence fills

Your beating heart, the only sound
That's makes you sure that you have found
No reason, ploy, or false pretence
Not to drink in, and drown, in nights silence

Create

I need to create
Or I need to destroy
No comfort in nothing,
And from something, no joy

The slate remains black,
Free from plan, thought, or ploy
And with nothing to make
It's myself I destroy

Close your eyes

I shield my eyes from the setting sun
Think back to days spent painting with clouds in
the sky
Can't help but feel I'm always on the run
Can't help but feel the need to question why

I pull my collar up against the cold
Remembering evenings spent holding you tight
Can help but feel I'm always growing old
Can't help but wonder if this is right

I wipe the rain off from my face
Remembering the times when I would dry your
tears
And now these memories feel out of place
With the pain that's filled these last few years

You and I were made to measure, built to fit
Until life's cruel joke and God's cruel theft
It's too unfair that I'm who's here to face it
As since you've gone there's no one left

Why did you close your eyes?
You know I just wanted to stare into them
One last time

It's 1am

Well the time is turning
But there's no tomorrow
It's just today again
And you're slowly learning
Through all your sorrow
To hear with the pain

Yet your mind is numb
And you feel the cold touch
As it falls through your hand
And you feel struck dumb
By just how much
You don't understand

Well the world's in motion
But you're stuck in place
Repeating what you've already done
And the crazy notion
A picture on your face
Is that you're the only one

You can feel the silence
Press down on your mind
It's forever, always there
And the only defence

With everything you find
Is to pretend you actually care

And you're stuck
Staring at the shadows and the darkness and the
picture of how each moment could be different
and how you wish you could have acted and
what you wish you would have said.

But you didn't
So you're alone and you're cold and you can feel
the weight inside your head that keeps you
locked into routine and with the motions that
keep your trapped within each day safe from the
notion that you're free but for your mind.

You want out but you're afraid
Can't face the fact that you're enslaved
You want to travel out alone
A thousand miles from your home
But you're locked in to what you know
It's all chains to make you never go
Can't fear the fear, not of it all
But just of stepping out your door, and just how
small
You really are.

And I wish I had a reason to wake up

Well Spent

Dig, dig, dig away at the ground
Who knows what you've found
Through the wails and cries
And the maze of your eyes

Think, think, think hard 'bout your past
And how the moments blend fast
And which path you should take
And which bonds you must break

Slow, slow, slow down all your thoughts
They're like a net and you're caught
Like a rat in a trap
From here there's no turning back

Stop, stop, stop trying too hard
Your record's already been marred
By your half hearted attempt
To escape from your own contempt

You, you, you should have noticed by then
That you were setting the trend
And without question or pause
They would all follow your cause

Shake, shake, shake loose of your label
If you think yourself able
Try to forge your own name
And accept you're to blame

Stab, stab, stab them all in the back
Be the first one to attack
Wash the blood from your hands
With all of your oil rich sands

Don't, don't, don't spare a thought for all else
Nothing exists but yourself
Think not of consequence
But only of money well spent

www.ingramcontent.com/pod-product-compliance
Lightning Source LLC
LaVergne TN
LVHW011309210726
843509LV00017B/2121